HOW TO CHAT-UP WOMEN

Stewart Ferris

SUMMERSDALE

First published in 1994. Reprinted 1996, 1997.

Summersdale Publishers Ltd
46 West Street
Chichester
West Sussex
PO19 1RP
United Kingdom

www.summersdale.com

Printed and bound in Great Britain
by Cox & Wyman Ltd

ISBN 1 84024 139 X

Cartoons by Kate Taylor.

Contents

SCENARIOS

Introduction

Men and women

Men and women have lived together on this planet for thousands of years, but widespread lack of understanding between the sexes has long been a major cause of disharmony. That's putting it mildly. In fact, the cause of every war in human history can be traced to misunderstandings between men and women. Hitler believed that Eva would be impressed if he invaded Poland; all she really wanted him to do was to shave off the tickly little moustache that made him look like Oliver Hardy. Saddam Hussein invaded Kuwait to impress his wives; they would have preferred him to have invaded the bathroom cabinet and set a razor to the rat under his nose. The First World War started because a certain Prussian officer couldn't grow one. Come to think of it, moustaches have a lot to answer for.

Think about the differences between men and women: there are the anatomical ones which enable women to have children, sit on fat bums and wear high heels; and which enable men to grow vast beer guts, understand cars and wear moustaches. There is the fact that women have a menstrual cycle that can alter their mood instantly (permanently in some cases). Then there are the *artificial* divisions resulting from sexual conditioning that begins at birth and continues throughout life.

Sexual conditioning ensures that men are taught to wear trousers instead of skirts, except in Manchester, and women are taught how to drive while putting on lipstick.

Men are just as conditioned to their own sex as are women. Men may not look in good condition for sex, but underneath it all they are all sexual bulldozers. Women, to continue the metaphor, are sexual window boxes. Try gardening a window box with a bulldozer, and you'll see what I mean. Women don't go for speed and efficiency in sex, they want to be poked around gently with a trowel. Anyway, returning to the metaphor, if you're a sexual bulldozer you'd better find a big window box to put it in, otherwise you'll never grow any seedlings.

Learn the following **Ten Inaccurate and Unfair Sexist Generalisations**. They are vital to an understanding of the opposing sex, and will form the crutch of an infallibly smooth chat-up technique that will be developed later in the book.

Ten Inaccurate and Unfair Sexist Generalisations About Women

1. They're all gagging for it, except the lesbians. (In fact, most seem to be lesbians.)

2. They're all mad. The word 'hysteria' comes from the Greek for 'womb', hence 'hysterical' means 'to have a womb'. Watch out.

3. Their sense of spacial awareness doesn't work as well as men's, which is why we have to park their cars for them.

4. They possess a 'washing-up' gene.

5. They live longer than men because men do all the work(except washing-up).

6. Their bra fastenings are designed by the same people who design the locks used in bank vaults.

7. Have I mentioned they all seem to be lesbians?

8. What have they got against men, anyway? Don't we respect them enough?

9. Women only think about having sex with their partner while they are doing it. This is the only time that men are not thinking about sex with their partner.

10. Women are all wonderfully different individuals and cannot be categorised or described by inane generalisations.

How to treat a woman

Use a good, durable varnish. No, just kidding.

Some men like to worship their women. They do anything and everything for them, shower them with gifts, think of them while they make love, and put them on a pedestal. This is bad for the relationship, counter-productive, and too good for them. The only time a woman should be put on a pedestal is when she's too short to reach the kitchen sink.

Any woman who is treated like a god will treat her man like a peasant. There needs to be a balance between what she gives you and what you give her. If she gives you a headache, give her gonorrhoea. If she gives you happiness, mental stability and bliss, let her off the housework once in a while.

Achieving this kind of perfect balance in a relationship can be as hard as Nelson's Column, but a relationship is like balancing on just two legs when you're drunk: lose that delicate balance and you fall into your own vomit. You have been warned.

Being single

To be young, free and single is to be a sad, lonely bastard. It's horrible, it's happened to all of us, and the only cure is to persuade a woman to go out with you. The right woman could come along at any time, but it won't happen until it's furthest from your mind, and since getting a shag is always foremost on any man's mind this means a long wait for most of us.

While you're still single, spare a thought for those stuck in relationships. Couplings don't work without compromise, and all those carefully nurtured habits which define your character and masculinity will have to be diluted. You have to be willing to make sacrifices, even with things as important as which films you watch: she might want to see a horrible romantic comedy, you might want to see a nice violent thriller.

So how do you cope with being single in the meantime? Normal practice is to develop a number of idiosyncratic, revolting and annoying personal habits that you can easily slide into whilst living alone. These will be a useful source of vitriolic acerbity, disparaging derogations and tautologous tendencies when you later enter into a relationship.

Recommended habits to develop whilst single:

1) Unlimited flatulence (farting).

2) Sleeping alone in a double bed so that you take up its entire area and all of the double duvet.

3) Always keeping the toilet seat up.

4) Washing-up once a month, whether you need to or not.

5) Bathing once a month, whether you need to or not.

6) Seeing how high you can fill the bin before you empty it.

7) Practising resonant choral belching for half an hour a day.

8) Thinking that flushing the toilet is the same as cleaning it.

9) Downloading an extensive library of prurient *art* images from the Internet every night.

10) Buying new crockery every month when you decide to throw away the dirty ones rather than washing them up, only to find there's no room in the bin.

Understanding women

Er, right. Yes, good chapter this. Very important topic. Understanding women. Definitely a good chapter. Yes. Well, I think I've written down all I understand about women.

Another attempt at understanding women

If women spoke French or Spanish, that would be fine. We could learn from a phrasebook what they are saying, and respond accordingly.

For example, she may say,

'Mon aeroglisseur est plein d'anguilles'
(*My hovercraft is full of eels*),

and you could reply,

'Je n'en ai rien a foutre'
(*I don't care* — or words to that effect).

All would be comprehensible after a few lessons. But women sound as if they are speaking plain English when in fact they speak a secret code which even MI5 cannot crack.

When a woman approaches you out of the blue and asks you the time of day, she is not actually asking if you would like to sleep with her. Believe it or not she really does want to know what time it is. When a shop girl offers you assistance, she is not making a pass at you, even if it obviously seems that way. What she wants to know is whether she can help you in her professional capacity.

Her are some common women's phrases and their true meanings:

1. She says:
Would you like fries with that, sir?

You think she means:
Would you like to come and meet me in half an hour behind the dustbin compound for a snog?

She actually means:
Would you like fries with that, sir?

2. She says:
Can I just have one pint of milk today?

You think she means:
My husband's away, so I'll be needing less of your milk and more of your renowned sexual services.

She actually means:
Can I just have one pint of milk today?

3. She says:
Would you like to massage my naked body?

You think she means:
Would you like fries with that?

She actually means:
Can I just have one pint of milk today?

What is required from men, therefore, is the ability to think and to communicate on two levels. Firstly, on the male, one-track sexual level which we are all used to and which enables us to cope with most situations; and secondly on a female level, where nothing is as it seems.

Communicating with women is like entering the crazy world of Alice in Wonderland or like trying to follow road signs in Liverpool. Don't be fooled into thinking you understand her: take everything with a pinch of irony, particularly if she is being ironic.

Conflict

Knowledge of the basic differences between men and women not only helps when chatting-up, but can also avoid conflict. Often, when couples argue, the woman will say,

"You just don't understand".

Too true. Men often make the mistake of expecting women to behave in the same way as men. Rationality and logic are standard fittings that come with facial hair and testes. With breasts, they are optional extras. But hang on, this is a little unfair. Women have their own rationales and their own logic. Their set their priorities differently to men, and that is why it's so easy for misunderstandings to occur. Put simply and objectively, only important things are important to men; unimportant things are important to women. Remember this when disagreement flares, and you'll be able to dampen the flames in no time with a broad minded, fair and patronising attempt at appeasement.

Useful tip: *listen to her.*

She may test you later. There's nothing worse than nodding politely during her monologue in the pub, occasionally looking her in the eye and smiling, while all the time concentrating on the football match on the pub's telly, only to be asked questions about her problems afterwards. 'So what should I do about it?' she will plead, just as the referee tries to break up an interesting fight.

You have two choices:

1. Own up. Tell her you weren't listening, apologise profusely, and join a dating agency the next morning.

2. Guess at what she was talking about. Her hair is a pretty likely topic, so if you say, 'I think you should dye it blonde,' at least you'll be in with a chance of salvation. If it turns out she was telling you about her pregnant pet dog, apologise profusely and join a dating agency the next morning.

Ideally, give her regular feedback throughout her monologues. This will make her feel appreciated, and create the impression that you are not bored.

Nods, grins, mmms, and sneezes will all show to her that you're still alive behind that glazed expression. She'll think that you're excited, riveted and enthusiastic about what she is saying. Women love good listeners.

When her monologue comes to an end, don't say, 'Hurry up, the landlord's about to throw us out.' Just kiss her softly in front of the fire . . . no, actually, that comes later. Find out how much she's going to charge you, first.

The basics of chatting-up

Most people find it hard to approach a member of the opposite sex. In fact, those who say they find it easy are probably either famous pop stars or liars. Approaching a woman for the first time is one of the hardest obstacles that has to be overcome in life. It is up there with taking exams, opening the envelope with your results, and keeping your drink down while you celebrate/commiserate. Unlike exams, however, success at chatting-up offers great potential rewards.

People are surprised when they hear that an incredibly attractive person finds it hard to 'chat someone up'. If they find it hard, it is to say they lack confidence. Therefore good looks do not necessarily endow confidence in a man. It really has nothing to do with physical characteristics: to approach someone you need courage, and this can be bought in handy bottles and cans at pubs and off licences.

Another common hangup is the difficulty in talking coherently to the opposite sex. You might find it easy talking to your friends but as soon as you have to talk to a woman the words cease to flow and you're left feeling self conscious and embarrassed. You lose control of your mouth and all the wrong words come out.

Instead of 'I'd like to shag you', you can only stammer the words 'Hi, how are you?' Your nerves have blown it for you. She tells you her name, and again you want to ask her for a shag, but all you can tell her is your own name. And so the conversation progresses. You really want to cut the crap and tell her what you're after, because if she's not after that you're wasting your time. She starts to like you, and thinks you're an interesting person, but bedded bliss doesn't seem to be moving towards you very quickly.

You try one more time to ask her back to your place for a shag, but the words come out as, 'I'm not the sort of person who does it on a first date,' because that's what you're brain thinks is in your longer term interests. 'That's a shame,' she replies, 'because I was going to offer you a shag. Looks like I've been wasting my time.' And off she goes. Happens all the time.

It's very important to control your brain and say what you want to say in order to avoid portraying an erroneous persona. But controlling your brain is just one of a myriad of things that have to be carried out simultaneously when chatting-up. Obviously the loins have to be dampened until they are needed, your body language will be under observation, and even the pace of your breathing can make or break the situation. These aspects will all have to mastered individually, and then combined to produce the polished performer that you want to be.

An excessive intake of alcohol will easily keep little Johnny Sausage from trying to make an early appearance while you're flirting with her in the bar, but it will rule out one or two interesting options later on.

Ten ways of dousing the fire in your loins until her furnace is ready to be stoked:

1. Tie a heavy weight around it.

2. Try looking at her only from the neck upwards (takes a bit of practice).

3. Keep the conversation topics *clean*.

4. Try looking at the barmaids only from the neck upwards.

5. Don't look at the way she handles her long, narrow glass.

6. Try to remember some recent sports results.

7. Think about moustaches.

8. Tell her it's actually a gun in your pocket.

9. Encourage her to be unpleasant to you.

10. Put a hat on your lap.

Body language is a major topic, and is therefore covered in a later chapter, cunningly entitled *Body Language*. For now, we'll just look at ways of controlling your panting breath on that important first date. Heavy breathing is fine in bed, but if you do it on the phone or while you're chatting-up a stranger, it somehow labels you as a cabinet minister (or *pervert* for short). Breathing is not cool when you're struggling through a first date, so here are some fatuous solutions to ignore:

Fatuous solutions

1.   Avoid any kind of exercise (even *that*) for at least a week before the date.

2.   Get someone to carry you to the date on a stretcher.

3.   Listen to soothing music on your personal stereo during the date.

4.   Die.

5.   Go scuba diving for the first date, and share your oxygen supply. This will regulate your breathing and can be very romantic.

6.   Get a job as a bus driver. When you see her waiting for the bus on the way to your date, drive past her. This will make her have to run all the way there. Resign from your job and calmly abandon your bus outside the venue for your date. She will arrive, ten minutes later, panting so vigorously that she won't notice the uncontrollable passion in your own breathing.

So where do you start?

There are no simple procedures that apply to all situations and types of women. Or breeds of sheep. Your *act* must be tailored to each scenario. With enough experience, life will teach you all you need to know the hard way, but why make the mistakes for yourself when you can learn from others who have already made them? Every time a girl lets you buy her a drink but doesn't subsequently fulfil her part of the implicit contract is a lesson in life, a demoralising kick in the teeth, and, worst of all, a waste of money. For less than the price of a few drinks this book will enable you to bypass those common failures and achieve more spectacular failures.

This book will be of use whatever your ultimate goal. It covers a wide range of topics from seeking a date or chatting-up someone in a bar to falling in love with a sheep or writing a drippy love poem. It will tell you what not to say, when not to say it, and when to give up.

Use and interpret this book, however, according to your own tastes, prejudices and bad experiences. Everyone has different tastes in women and it would be impossible to cover all eventualities. This book tries to cover most common situations and problems, and tries to show how most situations can be used to your advantage. The first part of the book covers different aspects of the chatting-up process, including your personal appearance and behaviour. These are the basic building blocks that can be used in the second part of the book in specific situations. These situations cover most of the common places in which we make fools of ourselves: bars/pubs, nightclubs, the street, parties, the office, holidays, clubs, the library etc.

There are no 'tools of the trade' involved in chatting-up, but one thing is always useful to carry: name and address cards or business cards. They are easily available from machines these days, so there is no longer any excuse for clumsily looking for a pen and scribbling down your number on the back of a bus ticket. Just give her your card, and who knows - one day, if all of her male friends die suddenly in a freak shaving accident, she may ring you?

Chatting-up is today easier to do than it has ever been, thanks mainly to a more liberal and permissive society. Imagine how tough it must have been for our recent ancestors: we're lucky to have been born at all, given the odds against achieving a moist coupling in the black and white days when potatoes, carrots and women were all rationed.

Psychology

This, in a sense, is what chatting-up is all about. There is a very fine line between a woman thinking you're a bit of a jerk but probably alright underneath, and her thinking you're a total git. What you say, how you say it, and your appearance are vital factors in swaying her opinion either way. If she finds you interesting, you'll probably need to change your sheets tomorrow. If you're boring, the sheets will have to wait a few more weeks.

.....then in 1973 I started my stamp collection.

You are particularly at risk of boring her if you think you have led a fascinating life. Try starting off the evening with a lengthy monologue all about yourself, about the famous people you went to school with, how fast your car is, and the story of your previous disastrous relationships, and see how far you get. Reciting your unpublishable autobiography to a stranger in a nightclub will bore her to tears.

Paradoxically, she'll come away thinking you're interesting if you have asked questions about her, and have consistently shown interest in her life. When chatting-up, never use the first person, always talk about her. If she asks about you, answer fully enough not to sound evasive, but don't use her question as a springboard to repeat everything you told your psychiatrist the night before when you asked him why you never score. Answer her question and then relate the topic back to her. She will probably have asked the question out of politeness rather than out of genuine interest, and will welcome the opportunity to start talking once more about herself.

Another cardinal rule is never to go on about an ex-girlfriend. Mentioning how attractive she was, how you never really meant to be unfaithful to her, and how every time you were unfaithful it actually served to strengthen your love for her, will only antagonise your date. If you must mention an ex-girlfriend, it will suffice to say how long the relationship lasted and when it finished. Avoid referring to the ex-girlfriend in a totally negative way: your date may then start wondering whether you would refer to her in the same way once she eventually dumps you.

Freud

Sigmund Freud did not have the benefit of a book like this when he went out on the pull. He had to develop his own theory, which was this:

Everything we do springs from two motives: the sex urge and the desire to be great.

If sex makes you feel great, then clearly these two motives are the same thing. This makes sense — if the purpose of life is procreation, the sex urge is what drives us. The intricate structures of modern society make the fulfilment of this urge a more complicated and subtle task than we are biologically designed to cope with. You can see examples of this difficulty in most pubs and nightclubs.

An important rule of dating is never to let a woman know how desperate you are. Drooling all over a woman will probably make her sick. It is all a matter of balance: keep the scales level and you stand a better chance. If a woman comes on strong, don't instantly fall at her feet, show a certain degree of self control. Then fall at her feet.

One inexplicable feature of women is that they do not always prefer a man who is kind, trustworthy and loving. Many women seem to enjoy going out with men who treat them badly, even if they won't openly admit it. This utterly bewilders men who try to treat women with respect (and there *are* such men around). The explanation for this strange behaviour has been attributed to the fact that women like the excitement and the challenge of taming a wild man. Sometimes it can seem as if you are in a Catch 22 situation: if you're nice to her she will find you boring, but if you try to act mean it could backfire and she'll dump you. But then again, travelling to the moon once seemed impossible, so someone's bound to crack this little problem one day.

Self confidence

Self confidence is the foundation upon which you will build your entire technique. Without self confidence your technique will be hollow. That said, no one really has genuine, total confidence. Even the most extrovert people have their moments of self-doubt. Your success will depend on your ability to fake confidence.

The problem with perfecting the confidence routine is that some women actually claim to be attracted to shy men. They often cite Hugh Grant's 'cute but clumsy' attempts at chatting-up in *Four Weddings and a Funeral* as evidence of this. Rubbish. If this was true, how come even *he* has to pay for it?

Most men (and women) lack self confidence because of the way they look. But ugly men can date beautiful women, provided they can afford it. Money will not necessarily generate sincerity in a woman, but it is a great aphrodisiac.

If you want to have the advantages of being 'rich' without really having very much money, it is possible to develop an image of wealth and prosperity on an average income. Good taste is the pre-requisite here: a slightly eccentric classic car, smart clothes and a refined manner. Save the beer money for opera tickets, read the 'quality' newspapers, and don't go on package holidays. (People with class don't go on holiday. They 'travel'.) Sounds awful? It's either that or going back to playing trouser snooker.

Image

Your image is the way people perceive you. If no one ever even notices you, then you probably haven't got an image at all. Don't worry — it's good to start with a clean slate.

For the rest of you, take a long, hard look in the mirror and ask yourself what image are you portraying? Are you, for example, the sort of sad, lonely, worrier who stares in the mirror at length wondering how they can improve their image? Or does your mirror swoon at the sight of you, forcing you to resuscitate it with a passionate embrace? Or can you see yourself objectively, spot aspects of your image that are attractive and those which might deter women from using you as a fun, convenient leisure facility?

Your image is made up of a number of attributes. Some are fixed and some are created according to your tastes, experience and class. The fixed attributes are there to stay, unless you want to indulge in surgical adjustments. But the variables will determine the types of women you meet, the types of women you'll never meet, and sort of pubs you'll get into.

The main component parts of your image:

1. Trousers. Whether or not you wear any at all says a lot about you. Jeans are popular, but their style, condition and fit can say completely opposite things about you. Streaky white stonewashed denim tells the world that you probably lost your sense of taste in a freak knitting accident. Levis 501s with a leather belt, on the other hand, will not deter women from your trouser area.

2. Hairstyle. Again, do you have any? If so, what message is it giving out? Hair is a surprisingly eloquent communicator, with the capability of saying anything from 'You'd better cross to the other side of the street before I start talking to you about my train set', to 'Single man, 23, loves sex, and is looking for any woman for romance. Must have good teeth.'

3. Shoes. What do they say about you? If your white socks are visible beneath your sandals, you could be in urgent need of a fashion transplant. Only wear shoes that are appropriate for what you're doing: training shoes are only for sport, walking boots are only for stuffing in the back of your car in case you run out of petrol and have to walk to a garage, and kicker boots are for kicking.

4. Hats. Best to stick to just one hat at a time, if any, and make sure you've managed to put it on

properly. Too many hat wearers these days do not own mirrors. This is a false economy: they put on a hat, have no idea how it looks, and spend all day wearing a baseball cap backwards, looking like one of the less intellectual characters from *Dumb and Dumber*.

5. Mood. What sort of mood are you in? Are you happy with your wash? Look closer . . . etc. Being moody is generally cooler than being happy, but it's not much fun.

6. Fingernails. Dirty or clean, short or long? And don't forget to think about your fingernails, too.

7. Dance style. Do you go to those modern torture chambers disguised on the exterior as nightclubs and rave enthusiastically to the sound of machine gun fire and strangled cats, or do you waltz elegantly (albeit alone) to your Sing-along-a-Strauss CD? People are attracted to different dance styles — usually it will be the styles you have never mastered.

8. Jewellery. Gold watch, bracelets, rings, and tinted gold glasses say much more about your taste than words can ever do, which is useful if you have a speech impediment.

9. Pepsi or Coke? Do you think it matters which one you're seen drinking? I don't think so.

10. Glasses. Big plastic ones, small wire-rimmed ones, or beer glasses? Which sort you choose may help determine whether you can see properly.

There are even more basic questions that you should ask yourself: do I have bad breath or unsightly personal habits? Filtering your breath through a gas mask in order to avoid causing offence to others is often impractical, but regular brushing of your masticators will help.

If your personal habits are unsightly, the solution is simple: keep them out of sight.

Here are a few instant turn-offs:

1. Unpleasant body odour
2. Greasy hair
3. 'Dull' hair
4. Dirty clothes
5. Unfashionable clothes
6. Picking one's nose
7. Picking someone else's nose
8. Scratching one's extremities

When inventing a new image for yourself, try not to stray too far from your inherent personality. If you're naturally a quiet chap, and you want to develop a 'loud' image, don't try to become a town crier all at once. Change your image gently by turning up your radio a little bit more than usual, and by complaining in restaurants at a sufficient volume for the waiter actually to hear you.

Everyone feels stupid with a new image for the first few days . . . but you're probably right to feel that way. Oh well.

Is it unfair that chatting-up is dependent upon the right image for success? Of course it is, but that's life. It's just a big act from start to finish — 'All the world's a stage, and I've got the biggest part' as Shakespeare didn't quite say.

Hide behind the right image and women will accept you. Get behind the wrong one and the only thing to welcome you with open arms is obscurity.

If this *acting* seems morally repugnant, remember that once you have attracted someone with your specially tailored image, you will then be able to reveal to her your true personality. And quite possibly you may also have the opportunity to start looking for another girlfriend.

Attracting someone involves selling yourself, but standing in the pub with a 'for sale' sign on your back has a poor track record of success. Selling yourself really means making yourself attractive to the prospective client. In a chat-up situation, the first thirty seconds of contact are all you have to grab her attention and win her over. It's similar to a TV advert: you are the product and the woman is the market.

What might your best selling points be?

* **No previous owners.**

* **Your rifle has only been fired in practice, never at the enemy.**

* **Fully housetrained.**

* **Inexperienced, but eager to learn.**

Would a woman become hooked by this sales pitch, or would you have to use a fishing rod? Try to make a list of your own points and refine them into a slick, glossy advert. Wherever possible, try to use these selling points. But if all else fails, get your rod out.

Cars

The car you drive makes as much as a statement about yourself as the clothes you wear. If you don't have a car, you're probably naked. Unfortunately a person is often judged on these superficial characteristics: you might argue that these material things are not important and you only want a woman if she will accept you for who you are. Well, that's your problem, but you might have to wait a while.

So what car should you be driving? Obviously there are constraints such as money, money and money, but here are some ideas.

* If you can't afford a new car, don't just get an old one: get a really old one. Classic cars are cool, cheap, and sexy. They're also uncomfortable, unreliable and difficult to park, but you've got to make some concessions towards getting a woman.

* Make sure you actually pass your driving test.

* If you have to borrow a parent's car, don't let it look obviously borrowed ... fill it with rubbish, play your own tapes and run it with the *fuel tank empty* light permanently on so that the girls you pick up in it think it's yours.

* Get something she won't be embarrassed to be seen in. This means avoiding metallic brown

Japanese saloons that come with a pair of slippers and a pipe in the glove box.

* If you get a Ferrari you won't need the rest of this book.

Mobile Phones

If you haven't got a mobile phone these days, it's probably because no one wants to talk you. Get one anyway, and pretend people are calling you at inconvenient moments by activating the ringing tone and telling yourself that you can't talk right now.

Size is important in this aspect of chatting-up — the smaller the better.

Self image

You must value yourself. If you find this difficult, go to an auctioneer for an expert opinion. Your value can be measured either in moral terms or in feet and inches. Increasing your sense of self worth is not difficult: if you have ever excelled in anything, try to bring that to mind before you begin chatting-up. This is not in order to tell her all about it, but to boost your self-confidence generally.

If you have successfully chatted someone up before but are nervous about doing it with someone else, boost your confidence by remembering how you did it the first time . . . and how the same disasters are unlikely to occur twice in a row.

Ten things you may have excelled in, but which you don't need to mention:

1. The highest pisser on the school wall.

2. Managing to keep the same underwear on for the longest without washing it.

3. Eating the biggest bogey.

4. Being able to belch and fart at the same time.

Belching and farting at the same time....how talented.

5. Not being able to get a woman.

6. Wondering why you can't get a woman.

7. Wondering if it has anything to do with the first four achievements (above).

8. Wasting days at a time wallowing in depression and regret that the first four achievements have blown all your chances.

10. Avoiding the number 9 wherever possible.

Your external image is important in making the first impression, but if you are a nervous wreck beneath it, or if you don't feel worthy of it, she will sense this and may lose interest. Assuming she had some to start with. At the same time, if you develop a cool image externally, this may reap dividends with your self-confidence. Try to make the most of your image and confidence: they are one of the great partnerships, like Fred Astaire and Ginger Rogers, strawberries and cream, and the John Lewis Partnership.

Fashion

Fashions come and go year by year, month by month and even week by week. Whatever is in vogue on breakfast television this morning is unlikely to be in fashion after lunch. This not only applies to clothes, but to music, cars, food and even lager.

So what has this got to do with chatting-up women? Well, if you wear a duffel coat and trousers that don't reach your ankles and wonder why people who follow the latest silly fashions get off with more girls than you, it might be wise to think about the shallowness and fickleness of some girls. They may, in your opinion, be foolish to fall for men whose only interests are pop music and clothes, whereas you may be knowledgeable about modern railway systems and insects, but if you want them to take any notice of you it will be necessary to change your style. Swallow your pride, your principles, and a few pints, try to look like everyone else, and acceptance by the female fraternity should soon follow. Lack of fashion sense can usually be compensated for by an appealing charisma and charming eccentricity, but this normally comes with age, along with incontinence and strange eyebrows, so it's not really worth waiting for.

Clothes

'The apparel oft proclaims the man,' as Polonius put it with characteristic pomposity. White socks and a suit tell more about you than a thousand words, assuming those thousand words were actually *about* you in the first place.

Looking good in clothes does not require vast expenditure. Don't buy cheap quality garments, just try to do most of your clothes shopping during the sales. Smart, tasteful clothes do not necessarily cost more than scruffy or tasteless clothes. Don't think that a girl will be impressed with you if you spend a fortune on a vile Italian designer shirt and then you say you can't afford to buy her a drink.

Girls tend to be more observant than men so remember to do up your flies; there is nothing quite as embarrassing as talking to a girl, then realising that your flies were undone and your shirt was poking out. Or worse.

Girls will also notice if your attire mixes patterns with stripes or if your hair colour clashes with the clothes. These may not be important on a global scale, but it is nevertheless best not to advertise the fact that you have no taste. If you want to play safe with colours and patterns, it is hard to go wrong with a kind of beatnik 'black all over' image, provided you don't end up looking like an SAS soldier and being asked to sign bestselling books wherever you go.

Whether you are hung like a donkey or like a particularly stunted mouse, tight trousers are to be avoided. Go for subtlety: leave the size and contents of your lunchbox to her imagination.

Attention to detail is important. A cheap digital watch on your wrist can ruin an entire image (avoid digital watches at all costs — just use your mobile phone to call the speaking clock if you haven't got an analogue watch). Jeans can be worn, but never with training shoes. Leave such combinations for children and foreigners. In the adult world, real shoes must be worn.

The Medallion Man, if you think that women find it attractive to see your shirt undone to the navel, with enough gold chains to supply the Royal Mint for a week, combined with a nylon chest wig, that's fine. It just leaves more women for the rest of us.

Hair

Long hair can cover up facial inadequacies, and so long as it's still in fashion and you don't need to be taken seriously at work or elsewhere it is a good idea to let it grow. As a statement, long hair says 'I'm unable to be original in my looks, so I'm copying everyone else who appears to be mildly trendy and I don't care if loads of blokes fancy me from behind', but don't let that put you off. If you play guitar then you've probably got long hair anyway, so it doesn't matter.

There is no point in printing a guide that tells you exactly how to have your hair cut. The only thing to do is to look closely at other people and try to get a haircut similar to theirs. Once you do this, make sure you check the current fashions regularly.

Otherwise you may end up like the thousands of middle-aged men who today still wear their teddy-boy's haircut from the Fifties, or the famous aging hippies whose fashion clocks stopped in 1972. Every six to twelve months is a good time to review your hairstyle if you have made it particularly fashionable. Otherwise, play safe with a short, neat 'business-like' haircut that requires little attention and is less likely to go out of fashion quickly . . . because it was never *in* fashion in the first place.

There is a bewildering range of hair care products available suitable for all hair types: shampoos, conditioners, gels etc. Although they may say they are for men, they are actually intended for women, only the *wo* has fallen off the *man*. Every real man knows that getting rained on once in a while is more than adequate to drown any unwanted squatters on your scalp.

Dying your hair is not usually necessary unless your mop is so dull that nothing else will bring it to life. 'Sun-ins' are very cheap, can be done at home from the packet, and will make your hair go bright orange no matter what it says on the packet.

The most vital thing to recognise if you are having trouble chatting-up women is whether you have 'square' hair. If it is combed with an immaculate side parting that shows a clear line of scalp from your ear to the back of your head, or if it is brushed straight down to your eyebrows in the same sensible way you have done it since you were a child, it might be time for a change. You may not want to make your hair 'trendy', but girls will otherwise perceive you as being square, which is the same as boring. They won't give you a chance. Get yourself a more outrageous haircut and give yourself a chance . . . to look really stupid.

If you are lacking in hair, a hat is perfectly acceptable, provided it looks good in the context of the environment in which you find yourself. If you are at the races at Ascot, for instance, you will not stand out from the crowd as someone who is blatantly wearing a hat to cover their follicular deficiency. But you might raise suspicions if you are in a swimming pool.

Facial Hair

If you want to have a moustache or a beard, make sure you are capable of growing one before launching some wispy hairs upon the world. Sideburns, bits of beards and designer stubble move in and out of the fashion spectrum like clouds in the sky. Whatever you have, so long as it's not blatantly out of fashion, you are marginally more likely to succeed. Even if you look a complete pratt, so long as some pop star in Melody Maker looks similarly afflicted that week, you should be OK.

Smells

Smells are used extensively in the animal world to attract the opposite sex, though not always successfully. The odd skunk also slips through the net when men try to put on the right smells to attract a mate — splashing macho odours all over can be just as bad as natural odour if it makes it too clear that you're desperate to score, but modest use of pleasant smelling after-shave may help. If you've spent all your spare cash on this book, just use water. It makes a good after-shave and comes out of a tap.

It is now possible to buy 'female attracting' scents in spray form, usually pheromone. These are the smells that tell the world that an animal is ready to fornicate, and it is claimed that they attract females to men who wear it. Females of what species, however, remains unclear.

Alcohol

The chances are that you're drunk right now while you're reading this book. Don't fall over. On the other hand, you and some mates might have decided to stay in and get sober, in which case you'll have to break ranks and get back to the pub.

Drinking gives you that little bit of Dutch courage that you need in order to approach a woman knowing that she will soon reject you in a vicious and cruel way. Booze softens the pain of rejection by enabling you to forget why you approached her in the first place, what her name was, and where you live. It is most effective in a rowdy party situation where you drink by the bottle rather than by the glass, and you can sneak outside or upstairs with a young lady. Avoid getting plastered in a public library, however, as it's difficult to keep silent.

There is less of a need for subtlety when the sharp corners of your amateurish chat-up lines are blurred by an alcoholic haze. Jokes are funnier, embarrassment is diminished, and the corniest and most blatant chat-up lines suddenly transform into aphorisms more worthy of Oscar Wilde than of Bugs Bunny.

Getting drunk is a great idea, provided it makes you randy and cute rather than violent and sick. Ask a friend which category you come under if you can't remember. Don't drink so much that you decide to drink a pint of your own urine, as this won't impress anyone. Well, it will impress *the lads* of course, but they don't count.

One of the biggest psychological blocks in chatting-up is the initial approach. A moderate amount of alcohol in your blood can make that first approach very much easier. You will be less afraid of the consequences of rejection, and will come across as more confident and less farty (provided you can still form a coherent sentence). However, this approach can backfire if you appear to be drunk and insincere. OK, so you *are* drunk and insincere, but *she* doesn't need to know, does she?

Drinks to avoid: anything with an umbrella or cherries in it. If you want to maintain a macho image, stick to pints. If you only want half a pint, but live in a rough area, order it in a half-empty pint glass. Otherwise, drink whatever you prefer, bearing in mind the suitability of the drink to the establishment: beer is fine for pubs, wine is more appropriate for restaurants, and intravenous drips are more common in a hospital.

Telephoning

Apart from the personal approach, the next most popular method of asking someone out is by using the telephone. Picking up the phone can be daunting; using it to phone a girl can be even worse. It's just as hard as asking someone out face to face, but at least you don't have to worry whether your zits are oozing puss as you speak.

Let us suppose you have met a girl and exchanged numbers. You will have given her your phone number, she will have given you her VAT number hoping it will throw you off the scent. Don't give up, track her down via the VAT office. But when should you phone after exchanging numbers? Should you play it cool and wait for her to call you? This is a dangerous psychological game, and usually lasts for about ten years. When she does finally call it will only be because she wanted to order a pizza and mis-dialled.

If you phone immediately, she'll be put off. It suggests to her that you've never had a social life before, and that maybe you could start it with her. Make her think you've already got friends to see and things to do by sitting at home for two or three days fretting, counting the hours, and desperately trying not to phone her until sufficient time has elapsed for your follow up to appear cool and laid-back.

Be prepared for the possibility that she won't remember you. She will probably have had fifteen men phoning her since the day you 'accidentally' knocked her over in the supermarket with your trolley and gallantly offered to take her to dinner as compensation. Have a copy of your CV in front of you so that you can remind her succinctly who and what you are. Don't give her too much detail however — she won't care that you represented your country in the Olympic Masturbation Relay Team.

If her response is clearly negative when you phone, don't keep pestering her on the phone each day until she agrees to meet you. Although in the old films the lover who keeps on trying despite constant rejection, declaring his love for her with flowers, gifts and phone calls, finally gets to marry her, in reality you will end up with a court injunction banning you from any contact with her. Learn when to give up. You'll get used to it.

If she sounds remotely pleased to hear from you, assuming she remembers who you are, keep the tone as casual and unimportant as you can. Don't make it sound as if your entire future happiness depends on her response, even though we all know that it does. Make it clear that you think meeting her again would be a great idea, but that it doesn't matter if she can't make it since you've got one or two other things to do. It's just that you can't remember what they are at the moment.

The conversation may be a little stilted if you or she is shy, so don't stretch the phonecall beyond a time that you can comfortably manage. A minute's dialogue can seem like a marathon if you haven't prepared a script and have difficulty in thinking and talking at the same time, so write down a list of questions and topics for discussion before you dial. It will take some practice before you choose the best structure for your 'informal chat', so don't worry if your first conversation goes something like this:

Her: **Hello?**

You: **Hi.**

Her: **Hello?**

You: **The meat industry has suffered from the success of European political union. Discuss.**

Her: **Who is this?**

You: **It's me. Frank. I knocked you over in Tesco's at the weekend.**

Her: **Oh God, not you.**

You: **Yeah. What's your favourite flower?**

Her: **Self raising.**

etc.

With practice you'll get it right. When people first get to know each other, there may be little in common to talk about. If a long, embarrassed pause occurs, wind up to the conversation quickly, going straight for the question,

'I'd like to take you for dinner at a restaurant this week.'

or whatever the purpose of the call is. Make sure there is a purpose, by the way. Note that saying later this week is less specific than naming a particular day, and reduces her opportunity for saying no. It is always useful to avoid backing yourself into a corner by being too specific about a place (she may not like it) or a time (she may be busy) when first asking someone out. She will then reply,

'OK, but can you come and pick me up again when I've finished?'

Use your brief conversation on the phone to find out information that may be relevant on a subsequent date. If she's a vegetarian you won't be wanting to take her to a Buffalo Grill and then on to a bullfight. If she's a classical music buff she probably won't want to be taken to hear your favourite busker who plays Beethoven on his teeth with a small spoon.

One of life's worst nightmares is plucking up the courage to ring her, only for the phone to be answered by a male voice. Try not to let your shock and disappointment show. Act cool, ask her who it was that answered the phone. If you want to sound really disinterested, tell her that her boyfriend sounds like a nice bloke. If she thanks you and agrees, you've got problems. If she says that you spoke to Hilda who has a rather deep voice, all will be well.

Reasons (excuses) for telephoning her

1) You're really bored because you've got no friends, and you think having sex with her would help to pass the time.

2) To ask her to a party. Clearly you haven't actually been invited to any parties, but you can always pretend it was cancelled at the last minute and take her to the scrap yard instead.

3) You met someone today who knows her and it's a small world but you wouldn't like to paint it.

4) You were wondering what size bra she wore.

5) She left some knickers behind when you last met (this obviously isn't true, but she might be spurred into jealousy by thinking she has a rival for your affections . . . and pigs might fly).

Where to go on a date

Where you choose to take your date will depend on whether you are better at communicating with words or with your body. You're obviously having trouble on the talking front if you ask her what her favourite film is, and she replied 'Kodak'. If this is the case, take her to see a film anyway and try to seduce her with bodily contact in the back row. No words need be spoken, no corny chat-up lines, just pure physical affection.

On the other hand, if she reacts to gentle contact like a cow recoiling from an electric stun gun, you're in for a verbose evening if you're going to talk her round to your way of thinking. If you take her to a bar, make sure it's a quiet one where you can hear each other talking rather than a nightclub in which you will need to lip read.

If she selects a suitable pub, make sure it's not one that is frequented by all of her ex-boyfriends, who are all fresh out of the army and desperate for a fight.

With most girls, avoid going to Halfords or a scrap metal yard for the first date (but think about it as a possible venue for a second date, if you get that far). Try to go somewhere exciting, like an airport, or somewhere fascinating, like a power station.

She may be more impressed if you offer her dinner rather than a drink, but you are also making a bigger financial commitment. Don't waste too much money at this early stage unless you really can afford it (see the tariff later in the book for guidelines on how much to spend).

Going for a walk is a great way to get to know someone, though check who you are dating before you suggest this option: you might spend the next ten years trying to keep up with Ffyona Campbell.

The ten best venues for a first date:

1. Her bedroom.

2. Her private 'nude only' swimming pool.

3. Her favourite lingerie shop.

4. Her bed.

5. Her silk undersheets.

6. Her silk underwear
   (while she's wearing it).

7. A Buckingham Palace tea party.

8. Underneath a silk parachute.

9. A Caribbean cruise.

10. Her.

The ten worst venues for a first date:

1. Your bedroom.
2. The local car showroom.
3. Raymond's Revue Bar.
4. Your favourite underpants shop.
5. Dinner with her parents.
6. Your local pub where all your mates are waiting for you holding score cards.

7. Her wedding party.
8. The beach where her boyfriend works as a lifeguard while on probation.
9. A motorway hard shoulder.
10. Your underpants (while you're still wearing them).

Handling the date

What could be more frightening than a date with a relative stranger, except perhaps a date with a strange relative? Dating a woman for the first time requires more balls than a bingo machine, so make sure you're fully loaded in that department before you go out.

Pre-date nerves can reduce a man to a quivering lump of jelly, which is fine for feeding hungry children at a birthday party, but will fail to satisfy the needs of a hungry woman. So before the date, calm yourself with controlled breathing, and try to maintain that *cool* image you have been trying for weeks to perfect. Believe it or not, she is probably just as nervous as you are. The chances are that an hour before you meet, while you're splashing after-shave into your pants, she'll be spewing up her lunch into a bucket in a final bulimic attempt to purge herself of fat that doesn't actually exist and which, if it did exist, would make her more attractive.

During those inevitable reflective moments before the date (when you're looking in the mirror), be realistic about what you expect to happen. Pessimism from the start will rule out any nasty surprises. The worst that will happen is that she'll hate you, and turn out to be a journalist writing a feature on the worst dates she's ever had, and you come top, and no one ever wants to date you again.

If you go along expecting this worst case scenario, you won't be disappointed.

Set a modest target for a first date. Rather than exchanging fluids with her, your target should be simply to exchange a few words with her before she makes a limp excuse for cutting short the date and going on her own to another bar to see if there are any *real* men with whom she can try her luck.

The next stage to aim for, if you pass the first hurdle, is to become a trusted friend of hers. If all goes well, aim for a *goodnight kiss* resulting in a *goodnight slap* after the second date, moving up to a *goodnight 'Oh go on, just a little one'* after the third date and finally a *goodnight 'Oh come on, you won't feel a thing, honest — I'll do all the work. What about if I pay you?'* after the fourth (and usually final) date.

When you do meet for the first time, how do you greet her? A friendly punch in the stomach or a groping bear hug? Or perhaps take off your clothes immediately and ask her if she would like a delivery of salami? In some circles a kiss on the cheek would be normal, but whether she will actually bare her bottom cheeks to enable you to do this is hard to predict.

If you kiss the side of her face on a first greeting, avoid nibbling her ears (unless you're really hungry) and keep your tongue in place . . . her make-up will be thick and fresh and won't taste too good. Be careful if you shake hands with her, as it can seem over-familiar, and try not to dribble.

If you go to get the drinks, you both have a few moments alone to compose yourselves, to let your first impressions of each other sink in, and for her to run away. If she's still there when you come back, the ice is usually broken by the following kind of dialogue:

You: **Er.**
Her: **Sorry?**
You: **Eh?**
Her: **I said sorry.**
You: **What about?**
Her: **Nothing.**
You: **Oh.**
Her: **Hmm.**
You: **Nice socks.**
Her: **Thanks.**
You: **Do you wear them often?**
Her: **Eh?**
You: **Your socks.**
Her: **Yes, thanks.**
You: **Nice phone. Is it off at the moment?**
Her: **Yeah.**
You: **Do you always have it off on a first date?**

etc.

When it comes to the end of the date, remember your original objective. Do you want her to respect you and give you a chance to form a long term relationship? Of course not! Go for it! Relationships that start quickly end quickly, so try to go out with a bang (or at least a little pop).

Before going for a one night stand, ask yourself if you're ready for that level of commitment. You may be with her for anything up to twelve hours, and a lot of previously hidden character traits can come out in that time. If you feel ready for such an adventure, the way you say goodbye at the 'end' of the date should indicate that this is just the beginning of something beautiful, something that will last all night. Don't let her get the wrong idea — that you don't want to sleep with her. Make sure she's aware that she has the option, and it expires very quickly if she doesn't take it up soon.

If she invites you into her house, try not to scream 'YES!' and dance a little jig up the front steps. She may just have a leaking tap that she wants you to take a look at. Once you've had a poke around inside her plumbing it will probably be time to leave. There's always a next time.

First impressions

Not to be confused with *doing impressions* of a girl, which is strictly for the professionals. *Impressing* someone is to print onto their mind a favourable image of you, one that will last long enough to override the memory of any disappointing facets she subsequently discovers about you. The first impression has to be a good one, so it will involve acting, faking and generally conning her into thinking you're someone other than your real self. It's dishonest, of course, but she'll be doing the same thing. Probably.

To take a silly example, imagine you meet a girl having just won an Olympic gold medal for setting a new farting record — her first impression of you will be of a champion, a success, and a potentially good shag. Now imagine instead that you meet her having just forced out an equally impressive jam tart in a public toilet, walking out the door with a huge smile on your face — she'll walk the other way very quickly.

Some men take it upon themselves to continue trying to impress throughout the date, in a self conscious attempt to prove their masculinity. This is not as important as it was in the days of our simian ancestors, since humans can now make use of lively wit and intelligence rather than swinging from the highest branches dangling their tackle, the modern equivalent of which is drinking lager until the bladder explodes.

It is possible, in theory, to impress a girl with your body, but it's usually not worth the risk. Keeping your clothes on until the last possible minute is probably the safest option for most men.

Performers are always popular with women. No matter what you do, being *up there* and doing something is sexy. Even the ugliest rock stars have groupies waiting to have their underwear autographed. A good performance of some sort always makes a good first impression. You could get noticed by the opposite gender by any of the following means:

1. **Talent contest — do an exotic belly dance with your beer gut.**

2. **Politics — stand on a soapbox in the High Street and rant about noise pollution until someone tells you to shut up.**

3. **Amateur dramatics — get your *part* noticed in a production of *Hair*.**

4. **Village idiot — become the local nutter who stands by the road all day miming a man pushing against strong winds.**

5. **Rock band — learn to hold a bass guitar and become a star in a string of pubs.**

Talking

Talking, regrettably, is a major component of the chatting-up process. It's where most men come unstuck. They've perfected their look, their smell, the way they walk (knuckles dragging on the ground) and they've armed themselves with a stock of infallible chat-up lines. But once they come face to face with the target, something strange happens inside the brain. It's as if the words they want to say get put through a blender somewhere between the brain and the mouth. So instead of coolly uttering,

'Shall we go and see a film?'
(To which she might reply, **'I've seen it.'**)

they in fact come out with,

'Shall we go and film the sea?'

Even if the first line goes smoothly, the follow up can easily become mashed, so instead of,

'So what's your favourite record?'
(To which she would reply,
'Sebastion Coe's 1500 metres.')

all that comes out is,

'Wibble wibble dribble.'

The words you say to her are clues to your personality, so getting those words right can be helpful. But worrying about getting the words right can make you tongue-tied and incoherent, making you sound like a railway porter. Then again, worrying about worrying about getting the words right can be even worse, so maybe it's just best to forget about it.

The main thing to remember on a date is don't talk about yourself. She's not interested. No one is. She's only interested in talking about herself, so let her do it. She'll love you for it. Prompt her to talk about her hair, her clothes, her job, her home town, her car (not in too much detail though - something along the lines of 'I see you drive a red car. That's a nice colour.' will be enough not to alienate her).

Ask what she likes to drink, what countries she has visited, what her husband does for a living. Resist the temptation, whenever she replies to one of your questions, to turn the conversation to yourself:

You: **What do you do to your hair, pretty one?**

Her: **I bleach it.**

You: **That's great. I bleach my rabbits: albinos are worth more. I'll cook you a stew one day, if you want. Tastes a bit like it's been marinated in a swimming pool, but it's alright really. Kills all the germs. Kills the rabbits too!**

Here are a few topics that are best avoided when chatting-up:

1. Football.
2. Computers
3. Cars.
4. Lager.
5. Strip lighting.
6. Stripping.
7. Fighting.
8. Trains.
9. Your wife.
10. Your diseases.

Don't you find the inside of a computer incredibly interesting?

If she tells you about her problems, under no circumstances try to solve them. Attempting to find a logical solution to her conundrums will result in you being swept away by her tears of frustration. Odd though it may seem, she will appreciate sympathy more than practicality. Just give her your full attention and listen carefully, giving occasional responsive noises such as 'uhmm' or 'yes'. If you can't manage those noises, the occasional fart will let her know you're still around.

Bullshit

Since chatting-up is all about making an initial impression and creating an image of yourself, it can be a severe disadvantage if you are a nobody who has led a particularly dull life, even by the standards of the other members of the local 'Dull Society'. If you are after a quick fling, it can be worth embellishing your curriculum vitae with whatever you think will make a girl regard you as a *better pull*. For one night stands, when you're away from home or on holiday and don't expect or want to see the girl again, you can adopt an exciting but entirely false persona for the evening - librarian, stamp auctioneer, or gas meter polisher. Enjoy yourself.

Keep the bullshit realistic. Don't say you're a paediatrician and then offer to sort out her feet. Basically, don't get out of your depth, unless you are such a boring person that it's your only chance. If you have to tell a lie to impress, try to make sure you can't be caught out. If caught out, laugh it off as a rather sad, practical joke.

When on home ground or when you want the relationship to develop, play safe and keep the lies small and white. Give your job a more exciting description:

'I work in the communications business,'

or

'I'm involved in the written media,'

instead of,

'I'm a postman.'

Bullshit also applies to your attitude towards her. She may be an opera buff, she may have a fetish for Norwegian fjords and spend most of the evening reminiscing about them. Unless you are cool enough to walk away from such a bore, in which case you probably have enough confidence and experience not to need this book, you should put up with her monologue.

That's so interesting.

Indeed, you should actively encourage her, asking intelligent questions about her specialist subject and pretending you have a genuine interest and maybe a little knowledge of it. Yes, you went to several operas last year (too many to name), and yes you love fjords too — your favourite is the fjord Mondeo. She will love you for it.

Sense of humour

Apart from obvious physical appearances, most women say that the most attractive thing about a man is his sense of humour, though they might have been joking. If you can make a woman laugh (at your repartee, not at you), it is likely that she will enjoy being with you. This does not mean you need to begin your evening together with a five minute stand up comedy routine combining sharp political satire with quickfire one-liners, but be lighthearted and make witty comments where appropriate.

If she has something serious to say to you, be careful not to say something you think is witty and will cheer her up but which she may interpret as insensitive flippancy. For instance,

Her: **I'm really upset. My cat died today.**

You: **Oh dear, that's a shame . . . all those fleas are going to be homeless! Still, at least you'll probably get a refund on the catfood.**

This is fine if you're trying to end a relationship, but if you think humour like that will win her love you might as well confess to being the one who ran over her cat in the first place.

Often the best way to share humour with a girl you don't know very well is to find someone nearby to laugh at, though even this method is prone to backfiring if you stray into political incorrectness by picking an *oppressed minority* type as your target, such as a Liberal politician or an estate agent. She's bound to find it funny if you see someone trying to chat-up a girl with a copy of this book behind his back, although she won't see it in the same way if she discovers *your* copy sticking out of your pocket.

Body language

We all know a little body language. At its most basic level we know the implicit differences between a smile and a frown, a 'thumbs-up' and a 'thumbs-down' or a slap in the face and a punch in the stomach. These clues enable us to understand a person's emotions or feelings. They make us feel welcome or rejected, happy or sad, without the need for any words to be spoken.

Wide, lasting smiles are usually more genuine than thin, short ones. A totally limp hand when shaking hands for the first time implies disinterest, while a firm, lingering handshake means she wants to have your babies. Listen carefully to the tone of her voice: is there a hint of enthusiasm in it, or is she talking in her sleep?

Watch out for hidden yawns, heads rolling to one side, and a blatant unwillingness to enter your *personal space*. She may defend her own personal space by placing her bag between you, facing slightly away, or by erecting a few miles of razor wire fence. Conversely, if she sits close to you and runs her hands up and down your inner thigh as she talks, it could be time to visit the family planning clinic.

Learn to interpret eye-contact. If she blinks repeatedly as she looks at you it's likely that she either has something in her eye or that she thinks you are something in her eye that won't go away. But if she holds you in her gaze, move your head closer to her and look into her eyes. The first one to laugh loses.

Physical contact

After you have been chatting for a while, you might start to believe that she will be receptive to your amorous advances. This is the time to think about your first move.

Your move has to be a subtle one, to make it easy to cover up in case it backfires, yet it has to enable her to reciprocate her feelings in a similar manner if she's gagging for it. This is where a great deal of skill is needed in reading those all important body signals.

Unfortunately many people interpret these signals differently. If you brush your hand against hers while you both stand at the bar waiting for hours to be served because there are loads of people in tonight and the pub is either short staffed or just badly managed, she might misinterpret your actions as an attempt to pickpocket her and will knee you in the balls in a most embarrassing way.

Or perhaps her handbag rubs against your bottom by accident, but you interpret this as a *come on* and start sticking your dribbling tongue in her ear, short-circuiting her tiny hearing aid and frying her brain, much to her annoyance. Be sure you have interpreted the signs correctly before *going for it*.

Timing is important. It's no use responding to her physical contact days later when she's already dating someone else. Similarly, don't pre-empt a possible move on her part with a risky one on your part (or even *with* your part). Respond quickly and smoothly if she makes physical contact by reciprocating to the same degree. Thus, if she holds your hand, hold hers. If she kisses you, kiss her. If she slaps you, duck.

It's not uncommon to leave a date thinking, *why on earth did nothing happen?* It was either because making that move seemed impossible or because she didn't fancy you. Usually the latter.

The trouble is that once the date is over, it's too late, so you have to be brave with making that first physical contact as soon as you get a chance. Making this move is tantamount to putting yourself up for sale and asking her if she will buy you. If she doesn't, you may be asking too much. Let her haggle, and see what she offers. Maybe she'll offer you a part-exchange on her ex-boyfriend? Maybe she was looking for something with a better fixtures and fittings, or perhaps a garden with a conservatory?

Rejection under these circumstances is nothing to be ashamed of. Well, it's no more shameful than any of the other forms of rejection men have to go through in their daily contacts with their opposites.

What body signs should you give out yourself? You can kiss her without warning and accept the consequences, or you can test the waters by some gentle physical contact, for instance by touching something *near* her.

Hold her hand if you are walking together (take her hand to help her over rough ground or steps, then don't let go — unless she trips and would otherwise bring you down with her), or rub her arm with your hand or with a roll of money.

Teamwork

It was Adam Smith who proved that division of the available labour force into specialist roles results in more women being successfully chatted-up. His theories have been applied and perfected by rugby teams who divide the tasks up between themselves into manageable chunks so that they can frighten and appal as many women as possible in the pub after a match.

In a typical team, two or three will be chosen to pour beer over themselves, another will vomit on his shirt, while three more demonstrate how to drink lager through their noses. A further two members will stand on a table and drop their trousers in order that everyone present can help them search for their lost appendages, while a couple more will sing songs that have no tunes, and no lyrics other than swearing.

In this way, all the necessary component parts of chatting-up women (rugby player style) can be carried out quickly and efficiently, ensuring that not a single man amongst them has the remotest chance of scoring.

If there are only two of you, teamwork can still be a useful way of getting things started. Saying, *my friend fancies you* is pretty corny, but it gets straight to the point without putting potential sparring partners in the ring together before they know they want to fight.

More subtle enquiries can yield useful information. A friend can chat to a friend of the girl you are interested in, to find out basic information such as whether she is single, how old she is, does she do it? You will then be able to begin your chat-up armed with a useful range of conversation topics:

You: **So, I understand you're single, you're nineteen, and you do it. Single, eh? What's it like being single?**

Her: **You should know.**

You: **Yeah. And you're nineteen. Wow. What's it like being nineteen?**

Her: **You may never get the chance to find out.**

You: **Cheers. And you, er, you do it. What's it like?**

Her: **I refer you to the answer I gave some moments ago.**

Teamwork and chatting-up were made for each other. With teamwork, the confidence level is doubled, the embarrassment level is halved, and the success rate is quartered.

Targeting

With the number of women in the world exceeding the number of men by many millions, we are, apparently, spoilt for choice. On closer inspection, however, it becomes clear that more than ninety per cent of these *surplus* women are over eighty years of age and live in a small mountain village in China. The remaining *surplus* consists of lesbians and nuns. But despite this, situations do arise in which men have the luxury of choice, and when this happens they must carefully *target* their prospective partners in crime.

When there is more than one female available for a potential chat-up, (if, for example, you have successfully gatecrashed a dormitory party in a girls' boarding school), spend a few minutes deciding which one will offer the best chances. The initial short-list will be dictated by your personal taste: her age, fashion style, number of teeth, etc. You must then decide who you have a realistic chance with. If this cuts the list to zero, start again and be a little more optimistic.

If you are inexperienced and are on a chatting-up mission for the first time, remember you don't learn to drive in a Rolls Royce. Save it until your experience gives you the confidence to go for that sort of person. You won't get the necessary experience, however, if you spend your time asking for driving lessons in that Rolls Royce.

When you have chosen who you want to talk to, and have made the first approach, work on her unless or until the signs turn negative, then target someone else. Don't keep flogging a dead horse. If she decides she doesn't want to continue chatting you up, it may be because the lights have come back on and she realises that she finds you physically repulsive, or it may be that she is meeting her violently jealous boyfriend in a few minutes and must reluctantly let you go. Forget her. Work on the next one, and keep your options open.

Don't be tempted to move in boldly on the girl leaning against the wall looking lonely. She loves watching her boyfriend win fights, and will flirt remorselessly with you until her boyfriend comes out of the toilet, grunts 'Hello', grabs your hand with his piss-stained paw and crushes you like a lemon.

Types to go for/avoid

When choosing a prospective lover, look for firm buttocks, strong shoulders and thick wool, not too tangled. Avoid sheep with horns or ones sprayed with the words *unfit for human conception*.

It's usually possible to filter out those who are *on for a bit* from those whose only sexual knowledge has come from watching *Carry On* films. Look at their clothes, their hairstyles and their general demeanours. Do they want you or what? Are they wearing wedding rings or fertility charms? Could your own charms make her fertile? Don't waste time and effort on raving feminists: they're omnipresent, but harmless — they just get in the way of a man doing his job.

Older women

There is a branch of philosophy which says all that men want out of life is 'Cash, gash, pie 'n' mash,' though not necessarily in that order. If this is true, it is often the older woman who is able to supply it. Sexual experience, confidence and financial security make older women such attractive propositions that younger men can often be seen queuing to do any kind of voluntary work at old people's rest homes.

Some women get sexier as they mature, others do not stand the test of time so well. It is rare to find someone who is perfectly preserved, except for some ancient Egyptians. An older woman with children makes life interesting, particularly if she turns out to have an irresistible daughter of your own age, or perhaps older. This kind of scenario is enough to put years on you. Her years.

Married women

Schoolboy:	**Sir, my girlfriend's three months pregnant. Is it safe to have sex with her?**
Teacher:	**Only if her husband doesn't find out.**

Falling for a married woman is very easy, but coping with the relationship is complicated. If a married woman sees you as her ticket to a more exciting life, tread very carefully. If you don't tread carefully, then at least take off your shoes before you enter the house.

Young girls

Within legal limitations, younger women are uniquely challenging. On the one hand they are inexperienced, inhibited, unworldly and unqualified, but on the other . . . well, it's just their bodies, really. A young body is great, provided you don't want to get a decent conversation out of it. Not that most men would be bothered by that, anyway.

Pretty girls

Going out with a pretty girl is great for the ego, and is bound to make your friends jealous. Until she sleeps with them, too. Chatting-up a pretty girl is always harder psychologically — it's like climbing a bigger mountain than usual. But don't be afraid of trying to conquer her mountain range, you may find that she gets fewer men approaching her than other women simply because most men don't aim that high.

If you decide to go for a pretty girl, just be aware that she will be used to being spoilt by rich boyfriends. If your four poster bed is just a single mattress with four Abba posters on the wall, don't bother. If you pester famous people you meet in the street, rather than *them* begging for an autograph from *you*, don't bother. If you would have to consult with your bank manager before offering to take your lady to Paris for lunch, don't bother. Impetuous, wealthy, high flyers best know how to treat pretty girls.

Ugly girls

Go on, give them a go. No one looks at the mantelpiece when they're stoking the fire, after all.

Teacher/student affairs

If you're slipping behind in your studies, this can be a great way to push up your marks. Those intimate tutorials, the hours spent close to each other talking bollocks, the sense of struggling together to bring you up to scratch intellectually — all this can pull a student and a teacher passionately together.

The trouble is that such relationships are often doomed to secrecy and a feeling of sordidness (nothing wrong with that, of course). Your exam results will improve temporarily, but once your tutor moves on to the next young stud you'll be back to spanking the monkey until it can't take any more abuse.

Sex

A tricky subject, particularly for men - who have to do all the work. Making love (as women like to call it) or shagging requires physical dexterity, subtlety, suppleness and tact. In theory men should try to stimulate more than one erogenous zone (their own zones don't count) at a time whilst 'making love'. This is not easy when you've already got one hand on the television remote control and you can't remember which hand's supposed to be looking for a button.

The adverts are coming up, fancy a quick one?

To make love to a woman's satisfaction, either hire a professional to take your place (there's an address at the beginning of this book) or switch off the television for the necessary duration. You'll probably miss only one or two adverts anyway, so it's usually worth the effort.

Making love is all about being considerate to the woman. Ask her where her 'pleasure spot' is. If she says 'Blackpool' you'll be able to forget about making love and try for a shag instead. But even when just shagging, try not to channel hop too much: women can get awfully sensitive about such things.

It can be fun to tease a woman during sex, perhaps by pretending you're not going to pay her. If you are inexperienced in these matters, the best approach when you get into bed is to be entirely honest. No woman who cares remotely for you will be patronising or unkind if you don't know which hole to aim for or can't put a condom on without reading the instructions on the packet (make sure you pick up the right packet — she won't appreciate you trying to make a soup at a time like this) or if you give her an ice-cream when she asks for a 69.

Don't be too adventurous on your first date. She may not be inclined to be tossed around the bedroom as part of your sexual routine. It is also unwise to unleash the full potential of your sexual repertoire all at once, otherwise she may demand this all the time (what a drag).

There will always be girls who remain under the impression that virginity is a desirable state — until they finally lose it. For men, the opposite applies. Virginity is a heavy burden for a man to carry, like having a heavy sign hanging from your neck that reads 'I am a virgin'. That is until you lose it, when you wonder what all the fuss was about.

Love

People say that 'money can't buy love'. Not for them, it can't, simply because they can't afford it. Love nevertheless flourishes without financial assistance among the poor. Love overpowers hearts, upsets stomachs, and causes diarrhoea in even the hardiest constitutions. Starting with *love at first sight*, love develops into strange, absent-minded behaviour, before finally melting into a pot of indifference soup.

So what is love at first sight? How does it occur? The answer is simply that it doesn't exist. It's actually *lust* at first sight, a strong, overwhelming emotion that is hard to distinguish from love. Lust is short-lived, easy-in, easy-out. *Love* tends to last a little longer. *True love* can last all day.

How to tell if you have genuinely fallen in love:

Toilet roll test
The most objective test is the *toilet roll test*. Make a note of your rate of toilet roll consumption, and if it increases suddenly during a seven day period then you're in love (either with a woman or with your toilet).

Size of your tip test
The next best test is the *size of your tip test*. The size of your tip will increase when you fall in love, so look carefully and see if this is the case.

The best place to perform the *size of your tip test* is in a restaurant with your lady friend. If you tip the waiter more generously than usual, you're in love.

Baby test
The *baby test* can be performed by looking at someone else's baby. If you smile at it, you're in love. If you growl until it cries, you're not in love. And probably never will be.

How to write a love letter

Messages of love are more often communicated by fax, e-mail or by sheets hanging from motorway bridges than by letters these days. The only letters that most of us write are to bank managers and these are rarely of a romantic nature (unless you have a fetish for numbers).

If you fill your love letter with romantic slobbering it will be too soggy to post. Keep it dry and crispy so that it retains its shape during its long, arduous journey to the doormat of your loved one.

But how do you *write* a love letter? Basically, you pick up a pen, and drag the moist end of it over a blank sheet of paper in such a way that inky shapes remain on the paper. These are *words*. Make sure you use the words *your*, *love*, *I*, and *jugs* in any letter. These are the raw materials of love letter writing, and can be used in different orders to tell her how you feel:

> *Your jugs I love*
>
> *I love your jugs*
>
> *Jugs love I your.*

If you can draw a picture of the object of your desires, then so much the better. If not, just cut out a photo of a similar pair. She'll be flattered.

For a romantic end to the letter, sellotape a pubic hair to the bottom of the page with the message, *there's plenty more where that came from, luv.* Wipe the letter across your armpit to give it a 'sexy' aroma, pop it in the post, sit back and wait for the response. The police will probably be around in no time.

How to write a love poem

Writing a good love poem is no guarantee of success with women. Shakespeare wrote some of the best gooey rubbish that's ever been written, but his track record with the chicks is certainly nothing to write about. If you need to write a poem for her, the best approach is to use lots of classical imagery. Drop in names of Greek and Roman classical gods, and compare the girl's attributes to the levels of perfection personified by such gods. Don't be tempted to modernise it and compare her to your favourite footballer or supermodel — she won't be impressed.

An alternative approach is to take an existing love poem and adapt it to your needs. If she's the sort of woman who thinks Marvell wrote superhero comics, you could very likely get away with this.

If you have to write an original poem, use her name in the poem, several times if possible, to make her feel that you wrote it just for her. Never use a photocopied poem in which a gap, which has been left for the woman's name, has been filled in with biro.

An ideal poem, **Ode to Jane**, is printed overleaf.

Ode to Jane

Oh Jane, Jane, Jane,

You drive me insane, Jane,

With your jugs and your newly flushed drain;

Oh how wonderful to be with you again, Jane.

Oh Jane, Jane, Jane,

When my funds began to wane,

I looked for you in vain,

And I was forced to explain

To my bank manager that I needed a loan.

But now I am no longer alone

Because I can hear you moan,

Reverberating through my brain, Jane,

Your voice as sweet as a sugar cane, Jane.

It truly would be a calamity, Jane,

If you were to abandon me again, Jane.

So don't.

How to write a love song

Instead of getting a tattoo featuring your favourite lady's name and an eagle, why not write a song about her? In each art form, tattoo and song, the lady is named, but the latter genre carries less stigma when you change your mind and fall in love with her best friend.

When it gets to the point when your arm resembles a page from a telephone directory, you may wish you had chosen to write a song for them all instead.

Love songs also enable you to write about the whole of womankind in one go — it's a bit like having 'I love birds' tattooed on your arm, only more respectable.

You don't have to be musical to write a love song. Ten minutes listening to Radio 1 is proof of that. Just buy a keyboard or a guitar, sit in front of the tape recorder and make some sounds.

Grunt the magic words, *I love your jugs* several times over, bang a saucepan unnecessarily loudly throughout the song, and simmer for three minutes. Serve with garnish and red wine.

Spending money

Chatting-up inevitably involves spending money at some point. It can become an expensive pastime unless you apply a degree of self-control over how much you spend on someone before getting anywhere.

Don't shower her with flowers and gifts right from the start. Or ever. You'll appear too keen and she will feel under pressure and will sense your desperation to keep her. (This is not a problem if she is as desperate as you are.)

Buy a drink at a bar, if you want, but why not be different and ask her to buy you a drink? If it works you might score at her expense, which is surely the pinnacle of achievement?

These days, many women will probably insist on either paying for the meal themselves, or at least paying for their share of it. Fine. And while she's at it, let her pay for your taxi ride or your next holiday. Don't bother protesting too much: women have pride too.

In terms of spending money a girl does not normally equate how much you spend on her to how wonderful you are. But don't let that distort your view of her. The following is a guide to how much you should spend according to how far you get . . .

£	Spending Guide £
£1	A kiss
£2.50	With tongues
£5	A kiss that she actually enjoys
£10	A bit of a fumble
£15	Time to change those underpants
£50	No woman is worth this much.

Take care not to overspend. Copy out that chart and carry it in your wallet (next to your selection of chat-up lines) for quick reference.

For other currencies, including the Dollar and the Euro, multiply the amount in the chart by 2, divide by 6, add your age and take away the number you first thought of.

How to act in front of her parents

Meeting a girl's parents for the first time can be a harrowing experience. Her father will inevitably be an army major with eyebrows that overhang like a pair of woolly ski jumps, who has an air of disgust that makes you feel small enough to fit inside the living ecosystem of his furry nostrils, and whose barking voice sends you cowering behind the curtains.

How did someone like that ever produce such a lovely daughter, you wonder? Her beautiful mother will be the answer to that question, and the cause of the next dilemma: you fancy her more than her daughter . . .

You will never be good enough for their daughter, so it's probably not worth trying. Whatever you do for a living, however neatly you dress or how well you speak, in the back of their minds will always be the thought that you are molesting their precious little girl. You are sullying their clean household, breaking up the family and destroying their daughter's innocence.

How can you possibly relax in front of them when you know this is what they are thinking?

Most girlfriend's parents will delve into your background when you first meet. Some will even have an *eligibility questionnaire* prepared for you to complete, the results of which will be pinned up on a wall with hundreds of others on their daughter's twenty-first birthday.

When staying at a girlfriend's house while her parents are there, the main problem is the sleeping arrangement. You may have spent ninety-nine out of a hundred nights at college sharing a single bed with her, but at her house you will not be allowed within a mile of her double bed.

There is nothing you can do about this other than sneak into her room at night provided the floorboards and bedsprings are quiet enough. However, show some respect to her parents wishes by making sure you don't get caught.

When things turn sour ...

What can you do if the girl of your dreams turns out after a few dates to be mildly less interesting than Radio 3 on a quiet night?

Do you take out a full page advertisement in her favourite newspaper telling her you think she's boring and you never want to see her again?

Do you daub her with red paint and drag her through the streets so that everyone knows she is impure?

Or do you take her to a restaurant, buy her an expensive meal, explain carefully why you think the relationship isn't working, and then carry out the first two options?

Ending a relationship without pain is like getting served in a pub on a Saturday night. Impossible. All you can do is to let her down as gently as you can, and hope she doesn't revengefully blab your personal secrets to all of her friends.

A good way to do this is to try a *trial separation*. You suggest a limited time to be apart from each other, say forty years, after which you have the option to get back together and assess the situation. This method enables you to get rid of her without actually letting her down completely.

Rejection by letter or fax is a useful means of setting out clearly and logically your reasons for splitting up. It doesn't give her the chance to interrupt and put you off, but it's pretty impersonal, particularly if you head the letter *Dear Sir/Madam*.

If you sense your relationship is heading towards a dead-end, ie. marriage, it's best to nip it in the bud as soon as possible before it's too late. Remember that 'marriage' isn't a word, it's a sentence.

Astrology

Your destiny lies in your own hands, right? Or just in your right hand? Men usually regard it as mumbo jumbo, but women are obsessed with astrology.

Star signs, sun signs etc. are all said to be connected to our behaviour, but no system of signs is able to explain why women read about their love prospects in their horoscopes before deciding whether it's worth putting on clean underwear.

Using star signs to match compatibility is all very well, but do bear in mind that it's all a load of bollocks. The only reason for including the information in this book is that women take it very seriously, and they will let astrological compatibility make decisions for them with regard to their preferred men. It's useful to know the enemy's reasoning process when trying to reason with them.

Here's a little guide to the basic characteristics associated with each sign:

Capricorn
(23rd December - 20th January)
The goat

Capricorns are usually called Jeremy or Xanthesis and live in Oxford. They hate wearing hats and usually sing out of tune at weddings. They drive a red car with a bit of rust starting to come through on the front wings which the bloke next door said he would fix but he never got round to doing.

Aquarius
(21st January - 19th February)
The water carrier

Contrary to their symbol, Aquarians never actually carry water, preferring to use a system of household pipes like the rest of us. They can be seen at night in their natural habitat, eating chips from a bag and talking eloquently about crisps.

Pisces
(20th February - 20th March)
The fish

Pisceans are 'vegetarians' who eat meat when their hippy friends aren't looking. They wear contact lenses (disposable ones) and enjoy sex with pillows and other inanimate objects. Pisceans are called Henry/Henrietta and they all live in a beige caravan on the Welsh coast.

Aries
(21st March - 20th April)
The ram

Arians like to watch television indoors on a hot day with the curtains closed. But in love they are romantic souls who will arrange flowers, gifts and soft music for any date, even if it is with a sheep. Their favourite football team is Cameroon, and they wipe their bottoms with their left hand.

Taurus

(21st April - 21st May)
The bull

Taurans are practical people who could build a toilet roll and a washing up liquid bottle from just a toy spaceship and a lunar base (using blunt ended scissors, of course). When not busy masturbating they, er . . . well, no one knows yet because we're still waiting to find out.

Gemini

(22nd May - 21st June)
The twins

Geminians are unpredictable. Sometimes they drink coffee, sometimes tea. Sometimes they take sugar, sometimes they bring it back again. It's infuriating, but the rest of the world has learned to live with it.

Cancer
(22nd June - 23rd July)
The crab

An ambitious sign which one day hopes to pass its driving test and get a milk round. Crabs have eight delicious legs, and are therefore very popular with shoe manufacturers, though their habit of walking sideways makes them very bad at queuing.

Leo
(24th July - 23rd August)
The lion

Leos don't like lemonade, but then lemonade isn't particularly fond of Leos, either. When not nude trampolining they enjoy nude cycling and nude shopping. In fact, they only dress for sex because it keeps some of the mystery alive.

Virgo

(24th August - 23rd September)
The virgin

What a strange bunch of bananas! Surprisingly good cellists, but very poor lovers . . . they don't know an erogenous zone from a parking zone, so be careful when they're parking their cars. Their favourite number is yellow.

Libra

(24th September - 23rd October)
The scales

The Libran rides a motorbike, and his name is Gordon. He married a female shot-putter, but the relationship didn't work out. She chucked him. Twenty feet. He's seeing someone else now, but she hasn't seen him yet.

Scorpio
(24th September - 22nd November)
The scorpion

Scorpions are invertebrate animals with a pair of powerful, pincerlike claws and a hollow, poisonous stinger at the top of the tail. An arachnid.

Sagittarius
(23rd November - 22nd December)
The archer

Renowned for their long-lasting bridges, archers enjoy country music and talking about sheep. Their favourite cheese is grated, and they rarely wet their beds, preferring instead to wet other people's.

There are certain star signs that are believed to be better matched than others. These are:

Capricorn	- Virgo, Aries, Taurus, Cancer
Aquarius	- Gemini, Virgo, Leo, Libra
Pisces	- Cancer, Scorpio, Virgo, Taurus
Aries	- Gemini, Leo, Sagittarius, Capricorn
Taurus	- Virgo, Scorpio, Capricorn, Pisces
Gemini	- Libra, Aquarius, Aries, Sagittarius
Cancer	- Libra, Scorpio, Capricorn, Pisces
Leo	- Aries, Sagittarius, Aquarius, Scorpio
Virgo	- Taurus, Aquarius, Capricorn, Pisces
Libra	- Aquarius, Sagittarius, Gemini, Cancer
Scorpio	- Cancer, Taurus, Pisces, Leo
Sagittarius	- Leo, Aries, Gemini, Libra

SCENARIOS

Bar/pub

Choosing your pub is easy in your home town. There will usually be one for students, one for under age drinkers, and one for single people. Avoid one that has a good reputation for darts and billiards. Go for something crowded where there is no room for sitting down, which gives you the freedom to circulate and to get close to a girl in a subtle manner. Excessive noise from a band or a juke box can make chatting-up difficult, but at least you won't have to say anything more adventurous than monosyllables.

The pub is often a good stepping stone to somewhere a little more interesting, like her bedroom. Don't spend too much money on alcohol in the pub if you have a bottle of wine at home and expect her to come home with you soon. Try the *false party* tactic to lure her home:

1) Ask her if she wants to come to a party with you.
2) If she says *yes* go to step 4).
3) If she says *no* go back to the beginning of this book.
4) Take her to a house that you know to be empty, knock on the door, and explain that you must have been given false information about the party.
5) Tell her about the wine at your house, and take her there instead for a private 'party'.

Nightclub

Clubs are designed for picking up girls in a communication-free environment. Chat-up lines are completely unnecessary, as are conversation skills, personality and musical taste. All you need to do is throw yourself into the heaving melee of vibrating bodies on the dance floor and see who you end up with.

Once your octopus arms have surrounded a girl, dance with her for a minute or two before moving in with that deadly tongue. Don't be shy — she doesn't have a clue what you look like, anyway. But just a little warning for those seeking a serious relationship: remember that the type of girl you are likely to meet there will be the type of girl who goes to nightclubs.

If the volume of noise in your local nightclub bothers you, avoid the temptation to wear ear muffs or to stick your fingers in your ears. Young women who frequent clubs lose their sense of hearing very quickly, so they'll only assume you're mad if you don't appear to enjoy suffering rectal prolapse with every beat of the bass drum.

Street

They're everywhere: you can't avoid them. Streets are such an integral part of our transport infrastructure that it's easy to forget what a significant role they can play in chatting-up women. Never mind the clubs and bars, the street is where the woman of your dreams is to be found.

Sod's Law dictates that a man who visits clubs every night, dressed like a million dollars, hair perfectly preened, body washed and de-odourised, will, in fact, meet the girl of his dreams on a Sunday morning when he crosses the road to buy a newspaper. He'll be wearing gardening clothes, covered in shit, and his breath will smell like rotting fish because he forgot to brush his teeth last night.

When you see a woman in the street, don't hide behind a parked car and oggle at her. Just walk by, calmly, as if nothing was happening, and give her a smile. Smiles are great because they cost less than buying someone a drink, and you can use them over and over again. If she ignores you, so what? You've lost nothing. If she smiles, she's probably just spotted her boyfriend walking behind you.

Introductions from friends

If you can get introduced to a woman through a mutual friend, you're virtually *in there*. You've got over the stumbling block that haunts so many potential chat-up encounters: fear. No woman wants to date an axe-murderer, and since such chaps tend to be somewhat lacking in the friendship department, proving that you have a friend will clear you of that suspicion.

Mutual friends have the added advantage of being able to warn you if the lady concerned *goes*, and if so, where to? You can find out her vital statistics (eg. how many A-levels has she got?), and learn something about her interests (eg. if she loves the Chippendales, visit your local antiques shop and find out when they were built, what sorts of wood they used, and what they kept down their underpants).

Parties

The dictionary definition of a party is, approximately:

> **party** (noun) *an event at which blokes get pissed, try to snog birds, and fail to direct their urine anywhere near the toilet bowl.*

You're bound to chat someone up at a party. It's as inevitable as cheese. Just take on board lots of liquid fuel, fire those chat-up arrows right into the hearts of all the women, watch them melt in the cauldron of your eyes, mix your metaphors, and visit the toilet every five minutes.

Parties in private houses are better than in rented halls or rooms because they offer so many intimate corners and cupboards. Look for a place where you can shed your inhibitions, rather than inhibiting your shed. You can go for a moonlit stroll in the garden, or explore the cellar where the light is conveniently not working so you have to *feel* your way around.

Other than getting into a cupboard with someone, the best place to chat a girl up at a party is on the stairs while she's queuing for the toilet. No one will be watching, she can't get away, and you're in there with a chance to break the ice with the 'Aren't you a friend of so-and-so?' line of attack, which not only gets her thinking but shows that you have at least one friend. Offer her some of the better quality booze you brought to the party and hid behind some books. If the main supply of drink is already exhausted, she'll fall in love with you for a few moments. Then she'll go downstairs and offer your bottle to all of her favourite men.

Office

Relationships at work can be politically complicated, embarrassing, and can disrupt the filing. Making love at the workplace means that paperwork can get knocked off the desk, stale cups of coffee are spilt onto the carpet, and customers look on in horror.

In the unlikely event that the chain of command above you is all female, it should be possible to sleep your way to the top. Once there, you will be in a position to help women from lower down in the organisation to do the same. Just be careful that the top doesn't get too crowded, otherwise you'll need a bigger bed.

Chatting-up a colleague at an office party is harder than it sounds. She already knows you quite well, or *thinks* she does, so the challenge now is to make her see you in sexual terms, rather than in *Marketing Manager* terms. Ordinary chat-up lines won't work here, so open up to her, tell her your inner most cravings, and watch her try to squirm away from you towards someone who isn't quite so annoyingly drunk.

Holidays

Chatting-up foreign girls is the easiest thing in the world, and is the best way to build up your confidence if you haven't had much luck on home soil. Where there is a language barrier, chatting-up becomes much easier. There's no need to say anything cool or clever (not much chance of that, anyway), and only the barest of platitudes need be exchanged before you can get down to kissing her. Without talking, communication becomes physical, so you're more likely to get straight to physical activities than if you had to spend half the night trying to convince her you were a green vegetarian before she would let you shag her.

Some package holidays are designed for getting laid, so take a good supply of condoms on holiday, just in case. Foreign ones may not be so easy to come by (or in).

Wherever you go, remember that foreigners will judge your country by your appearance and behaviour, so wear union jack shorts at all times, swear loudly in English, and always throw up in public places.

Swimming

Swimming involves meeting women who are virtually naked, which is great. It also involves exposing your own flesh to them, which is not so great. And you have to get wet, which can be a drag, particularly if you're trying to keep your cigarette alight.

Here are the types of women you might encounter while swimming:

1. Blubbery whales.
2. Mermaids.
3. Minnows.
4. Wrecks.
5. Old car tyres.

Mermaids are extremely rare, but the other four varieties are abundant in most swimming pools and other damp geographical recesses. Don't feign drowning in a public swimming emporium: a blubbery whale is more likely to resuscitate you than a *Baywatch* babe. Especially in California.

If you're not happy with the *unwrapped goods* on offer, try tempting a clothed landlubber with an offer of impromptu skinny dipping. This will inevitably provoke a tirade of excuses, some of which you can counter in the following ways:

Her reasons not to go skinny dipping with you:	Your solution:
She hasn't got her swimming costume.	She doesn't need it.
She hasn't got her towel.	Keep a set of towels in the boot of your car.
It's too cold.	It's warmer in the sea.
People might see her even though it's dark.	Cover her with Marmite.
She can't swim.	Give her lessons in her bath.

If all else fails, get a job as a pool lifeguard, and spend all day sitting on a high chair with a towel over your lap.

Clubs and societies

The sort of society you join will determine the type of woman you meet. Volunteering yourself for the *Women's Amateur Blow-job Society* (WABS) will yield entirely different results to a Thursday evening spent burning untidy badgers with the *Zealots Institute for Tidy Sets* (ZITS).

Look in your local paper for a list of societies and when they meet, and go to a meeting to see what the girls are like. If you're not impressed, just say so and go somewhere else.

Whether you join a stamp collectors' club (people who lick stamps) or a dog lovers' society (people who lick dogs) you're going to meet people of similar interests or lack of interests.

The gym

Some reasons why gyms are not ideal places for chatting-up women:

1. The women are always fitter than you, so it's impossible to show off. If you can do five minutes on the bike, they can do thirty (at double the pace).

2. The gorilla lifting most of the gym in his left hand is bound to be going out with the beauty in the transparent leotard who's attention you are trying to attract with your energetic endeavours.

3. The women will see you either as Mr Puniverse or as Mr Lardiverse compared to the *real* sportsmen who attract them to the gym.

4. If you come on too strongly, a rejection from a super-fit woman could land you in hospital for weeks.

5. You have to give up lager and chips. Is any woman worth it?

Library

If you are a student, you may be aware that your college has a library. Ask someone to tell you where it is, then go along with some books and a pen and seat yourself in view of some swotty, but pretty, girls, and pretend to work. The library has its own unique atmosphere, which engenders a sense of boredom and desperation in those who frequent it, so most girls there will be pleased to be distracted by you.

If you go to the library often you will find that most girls sit in roughly the same seat every day or every evening, and if you regularly sit near to them they will get to recognise and know you. From that stage it can be possible to break for lunch at the same time as them, or to walk them home, perhaps asking for shelter under her umbrella if it's raining (girls who live in libraries are very sensible and are bound to have an umbrella). The library is not a hunting ground that will give you an instant result, but given time you can develop some meaningful relationships with the desks.

Non-students can also use this approach either in a public library or in a student library if they can dress scruffily enough to pass as a student and get in.

Supermarket

One of the best, but underrated, venues for finding true love is the supermarket. Most people eat food, and most of them have to go out and buy it, so get your shopping trousers on and see what's on special offer.

Accidental trolley bump
This is the best supermarket tactic. It never fails to attract the attention of the object of your desire, if not the supermarket security fascist as well. Be careful not to nudge too hard, just enough to justify swapping insurance details and phone numbers. Remember that the police must be informed if anyone is injured.

Detective work
Once you've spotted a desirable dish, observe what is in her basket or trolley. The contents can give clues to her marital status etc. If she has children, you will see lots of dinosaur drinks, mini mars bars and nappies. If she is trying to avoid having children you should see a pile of prophylactics. What you really want to see, however, are ready made meals for one.

Cookery question
Pretend to be planning a meal, and ask her if she thinks you've got all the right ingredients. If she says you're lacking in the sausage department, find someone else. If you're lucky, though, she'll help you find all the necessary ingredients, cook the meal, eat it with you, wash up afterwards, then shag you. And not necessarily in that order.

Checkout technique
Follow her to the checkout, and help her unload her trolley. Chat about her food, cookery, the weather, and her plans for this evening. Then find another queue for yourself once her husband arrives.

Public transport

Trains are great places for meeting women. It should be easy to start off a conversation in this scenario: chat to her about the wrong type of snow, leaves on the line, recent rail crashes, and the Great Train Robbery. Ignite a fiery sexual fantasy in her by pointing out that if the train stops suddenly you'll be thrown onto the protection of her ample bosom, then ask her if she dares you to pull the emergency stop cord, and whether she would like to pull your own *emergency stop cord*. Then do whatever the railway policeman asks you if you want to avoid a hefty fine.

Chatting-up someone on the bus is not allowed, unless you're wearing a heavy disguise. There's no glamour in bus travel, so it's not conducive to kindling romance. Unless it's an airport bus. If you're making a long haul flight, try to enrol your neighbour in the famous *mile high club*. Airliners are perfect for engendering a sense of excitement and carefree sexual abandon. Asking your neighbour on the top deck of a bus if she wants to join the fifteen foot high club is not likely to produce the same results.

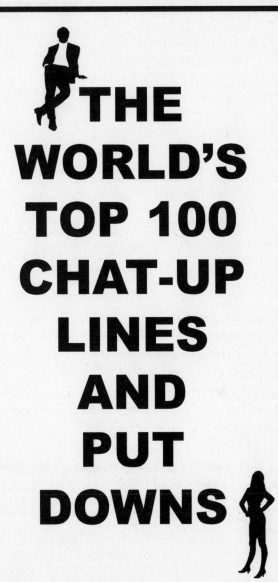

THE WORLD'S TOP 100 CHAT-UP LINES AND PUT DOWNS

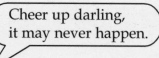

Cheer up darling, it may never happen.

It just has.

Would you like to perform sex with me?

I don't think I'm up to a performance, but I could manage a rehearsal.

Will you sleep with me?

No, I'm an insomniac.

I'm a photographer for a model agency: I've been looking for a face like yours.

I'm a plastic surgeon. I've been looking for a face like yours.

How would you like your eggs in the morning?

Unfertilised, mate. Piss off.

Are you separated?

No, it's just the way I walk.

Would you like my ship to sail into your port?

No. It's an airport.

Have you ever done it with a real man?

No, why - have you?

With you I've finally found what I've been looking for in life.

With you I've finally lost it.

I'm a doctor: what's your appendix doing tonight? I'd love to take it out.

Very funny. You should be on the television — then I could turn you off.

Hi. I'm on a computer date, actually, but the computer hasn't shown up. Do you want to join me instead?

No, I never date men with tiny peripherals.

Hello. Didn't we sleep together once? Or was it twice?

*It must have been once.
I never make the same mistake twice.*

Have you got any Irish in you? Would you like some?

Yes please. Mine's a Guinness.

Did you know that men with the biggest dicks have the smallest mouths?

I could park my car in your mouth.

Before I buy you a drink, can you tell me if you like me?

Get the drink first. We'll deal with the bad news later.

On a scale of one to ten, you have been voted ten by everyone over there. How do you feel?

I use my fingertips.

Please take a seat.

Where to?

How did you get to be so beautiful?

I must have been given your share.

Queuing is so boring, don't you find?

It is now.

Ring me sometime. Must dash now, but here's my number.

Don't you have a name?

The trouble with this place is some of the people that come here.

Do something about it — leave.

What do you think of the music here?

Better than the company.

Very nice gear you've got on.

Yeah, and it's staying on.

Are your legs tired? You've been running through my mind all day.

Yeah — I was looking for a brain cell.

Is it hot in here or is it just you?

It's hot.

Let's skip the awkward beginning and pretend that we have known each other for a while. So, how's your Mum?

She told me I wasn't to see you anymore.

I'm not interested in a relationship, but I don't feel like being alone tonight.

Are you asking for a shag, or what?

You're just my type — you're a girl.

I'm just my type as well, I'm afraid.

I'd go to the ends of the world for you.

Yes, but would you stay there?

Can I have your phone number?

No, but you can have my dialling code.

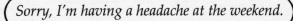

Will you come out with me on Saturday?

Sorry, I'm having a headache at the weekend.

You're the kind of girl I'd like to take home to mother except I can't trust my father.

Don't worry – he's not the sort to drink from the same cup twice.

Your face must turn a few heads.

Yours must turn a few stomachs.

I'm pleased to tell you that we've held a competition and you've won my heart.

First prize and booby prize all rolled into one.

Go on, don't be shy: ask me out.

OK, get out.

Hi. I'm a tenor.

Sorry, I've only got a fiver.

You don't sweat much for a fat lass.

I will when I start running away from you.

I'd like to see more of you.

There isn't any more of me.

Do you kiss with your eyes closed?

I would if I were kissing you.

I think I could make you very happy.

Why, are you leaving?

You would be great to go on a camping holiday with. Separate tents, of course.

I'd prefer separate campsites.

Is there anything I can do for you?

I doubt it. There was obviously nothing you could do for yourself.

You seem to me like a sensible girl.

That's right — I won't go anywhere near you.

Do you mind if I smoke?

I don't care if you burn.

Can I kiss you?

Of course, but mind you don't burn yourself on my cigarette.

What would you say if I asked you to marry me?

Nothing. I can't talk and laugh at the same time.

I'm a meteorologist, and I'd like to study your warm front. Let's go to an isobar and have a drink.

No thanks — I've seen the forecast. Damp in parts, hot and sticky with rising cumulo nimbus. I think I'll stay at home.

I've circumnavigated the world single-handed.

What were you doing with your other hand, then?

How can I prove my love for you?

In a court of law.

What would you say is my best feature?

Your ornamental pond.

Shall we go all the way?

Yes, as long as it's in different directions.

Do you think you could fall for me?

Only if you pushed me.

Don't go — you'll never find anyone like me again.

I certainly hope not.

Can I have your name?

Why — haven't you already got one?

Tell me your star sign.

Virgo. Intactus.

Shall we go and see a film?

I've seen it.

When I look at the stars I see your eyes. When I look at a flower I smell your perfume. When I look at the sun I feel your warmth.

When I look at a cow I see your bullshit.

When I roll across my satin sheets at night, the sound reminds me of you.

What, while I'm eating a packet of crisps?

Do you think it was fate that brought us together?

No. It was just bad luck.

If I had known I was going to meet someone as amazingly lovely as you, I'd have had my nostrils plucked.

And if I'd known I was going to meet someone as ugly as you, I'd have had my eyeballs plucked.

Am I ever in your dreams?

No, only in my nightmares.

I'm afraid I'm an incurable romantic.

Well, you're incurable, that's for sure.

Why are you drinking with such a tiny straw?

It reminds me of you.

I'm feeling a bit depressed.
Have you got any advice?

Yes, bloody cheer up.

It's great that we met here tonight.
Why don't we meet up again?

Because I don't want to.

Would you accept if I were to ask you out?

Accept what — defeat?

The pillar outside this building symbolises my feelings for you.

You've just trod in the stuff that symbolises my feelings for you.

You know what I like most about you? All of you.

That's great, because I'm an all or nothing sort of person, and with you it's nothing.

Don't go away
— I'm just going to put the kettle on.

Are you sure it will fit you?

Do you do any charity work?

Yes, usually to help people like you.

Try imagining you're in love with me.

My imagination doesn't stretch that far.

My name's Russell — you can hear me coming.

*I'm Ivy
— but I don't think I'll grow on you.*

Will you go out with me? My name's Roger.

Sorry, I don't fancy being Rogered tonight.

The name's Thomas, John Thomas.

*That's OK, I'm Holly,
so I'm used to little pricks.*

Can I have a tinkle on your piano?

I'd rather you used the toilet.

Can I introduce you to my dog, Raffles?

Oh, isn't he big? Can I stroke him?

Of course. Would you like to stroke Raffles as well?

I want people to love me for myself, not my money.

Isn't that narrowing your options somewhat?

Have you had a wonderful evening?

Sure, but it wasn't this one.

How deeply do you feel for me?

About sewer level.

Would you go to bed with a perfect stranger?

Yes — but you're not perfect.

What would I have to give you to get a little kiss?

Chloroform.

You've got the face of an angel.

And you've got the face of a saint — a Saint Bernard.

I've always believed in love at first sight.

So did I — until I met you.

My ideal woman has to have a great sense of humour.

That will have to be the only sense she has.

Hi there. I'd like to ask you what's your idea of a perfect evening?

The one I was having before you came over.

What's your favourite flower?

Self-raising.

What's your favourite record?

Sebastian Coe's 1500 metres.

What do you normally
listen to in the evenings?

Prats like you.

What's your favourite group?

The backbench 1922 committee.

Where shall we go for our honeymoon?

What about Finland?
And I'll go to New Zealand.

I'd run a four minute mile for you.

I'd run a four minute mile from you.

Do you realise that I'm just a stick of sexual dynamite?

You mean once your fuse is lit you explode within five seconds?

What's your favourite film?

Kodak.

What's your favourite French dish?

Eric Cantona.

Do you have a favourite singer?

Yes, the ones with two bobbins and a foot pedal.

Am I everything you thought I'd be?

Yes, everything and worse.

Epilogue

To end this book I would like to summarise a few important points. Being single is the not the end of the world, but it's dangerously close to Outer Mongolia. Eight out of ten philosophers agree that the most important thing in life is to be happy. Eight out of ten mechanics agree that the second most important thing is to service your car regularly. In third place, it is vital to service your relationship every 12,000 miles. Remember that being in a relationship will not automatically bring happiness, but if regularly maintained it should give you years of trouble-free rides.

Relationships and playing the game of forming relationships can be fun. Whether you are meeting girls through dating agencies, mutual friends or as strangers in a pub, have fun. And if she won't let you have fun, she's probably just practising for when you get married.

**Here are some *don'ts*
to send you on your merry way:**

1. Don't be square but don't be so fashionable
   that your clothes appear to be inside out and
   your hair looks like a toilet brush.

2. Don't force your attentions on her but don't
   simply force them on yourself each night,
   either.

3. Don't excessively flatter her but don't throw a
   bucket of paint over her.

4. Don't have unpleasant body odour but don't
   wear so much after-shave that you smell like a
   perfume factory.

5. Don't talk about yourself all evening but don't
   be so moody and silent that she guesses you've
   got something to hide.

6. Don't be flashy but don't be dull.

7. Don't dismiss what she talks about as trivial but don't pander obsequiously to her every word.

8. Don't mention how well you get on with the nurses at the local VD clinic, but don't bother showing her the results of a recent medical to prove you're up to the job.

9. Don't panic!

10. Don't think for a moment that anything in this book will actually improve your chances!